Adult Coloring Book

CONTENTMENT

Stress Relieving Patterns

Joyce Mitchell

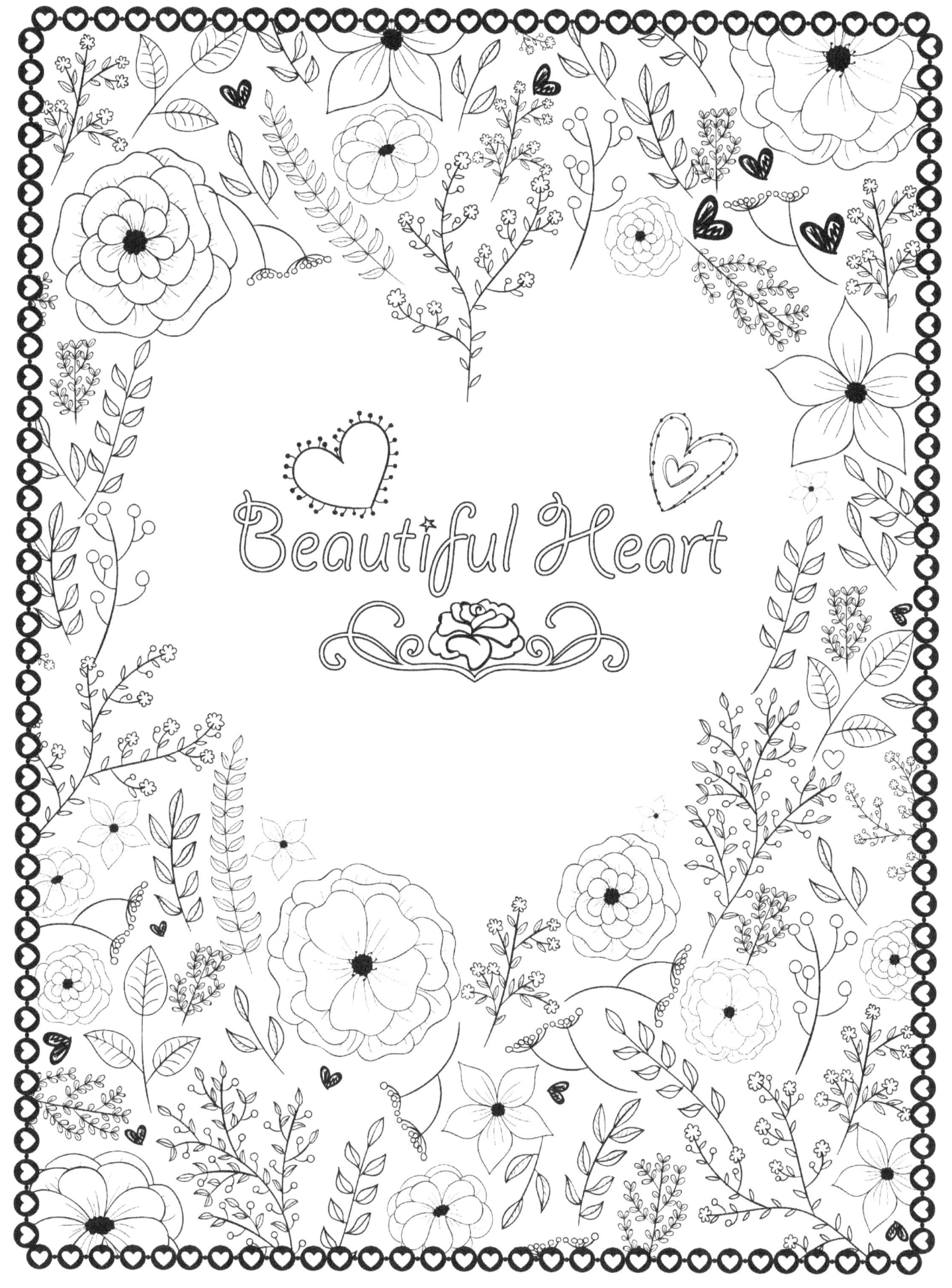

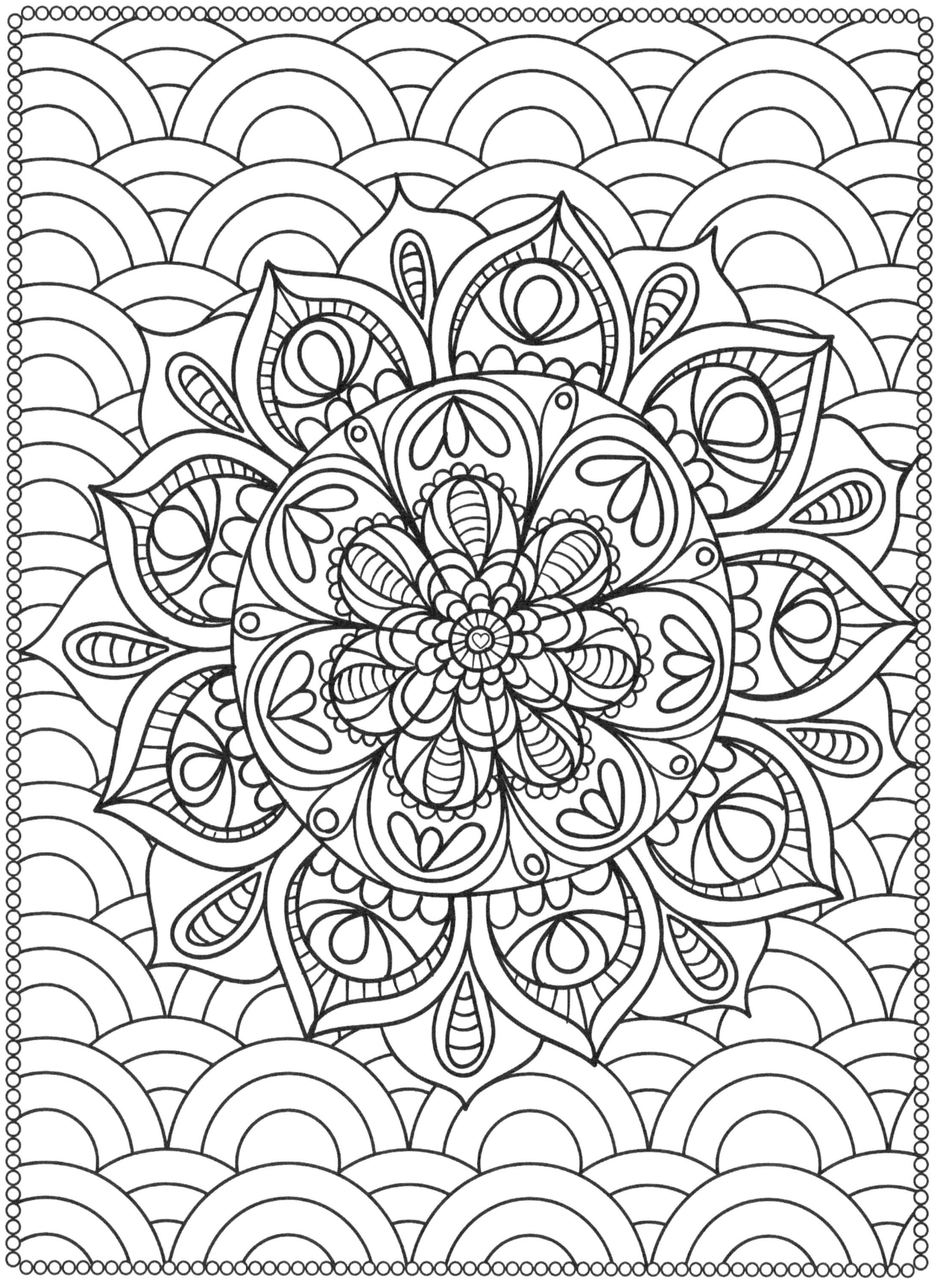

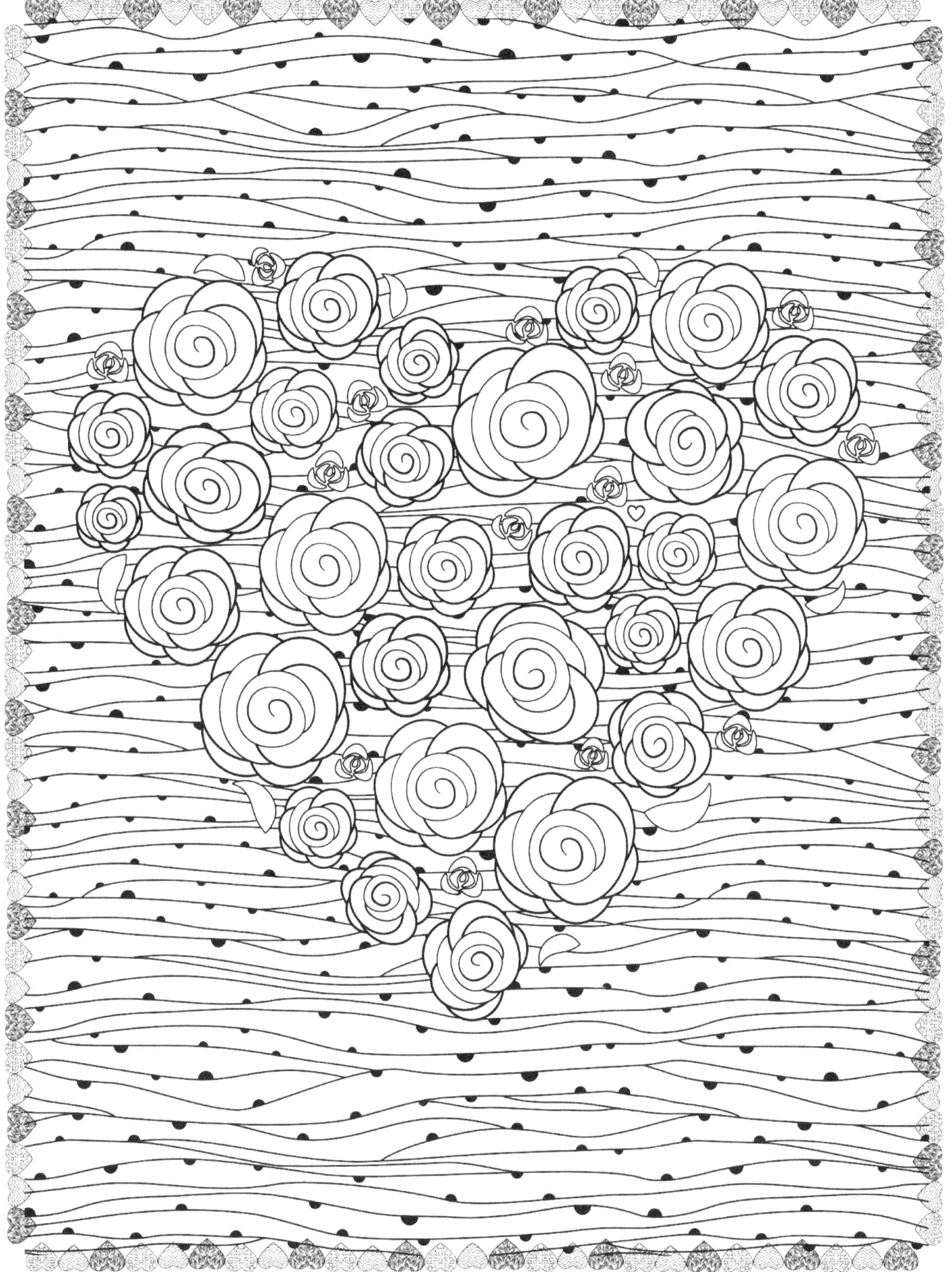

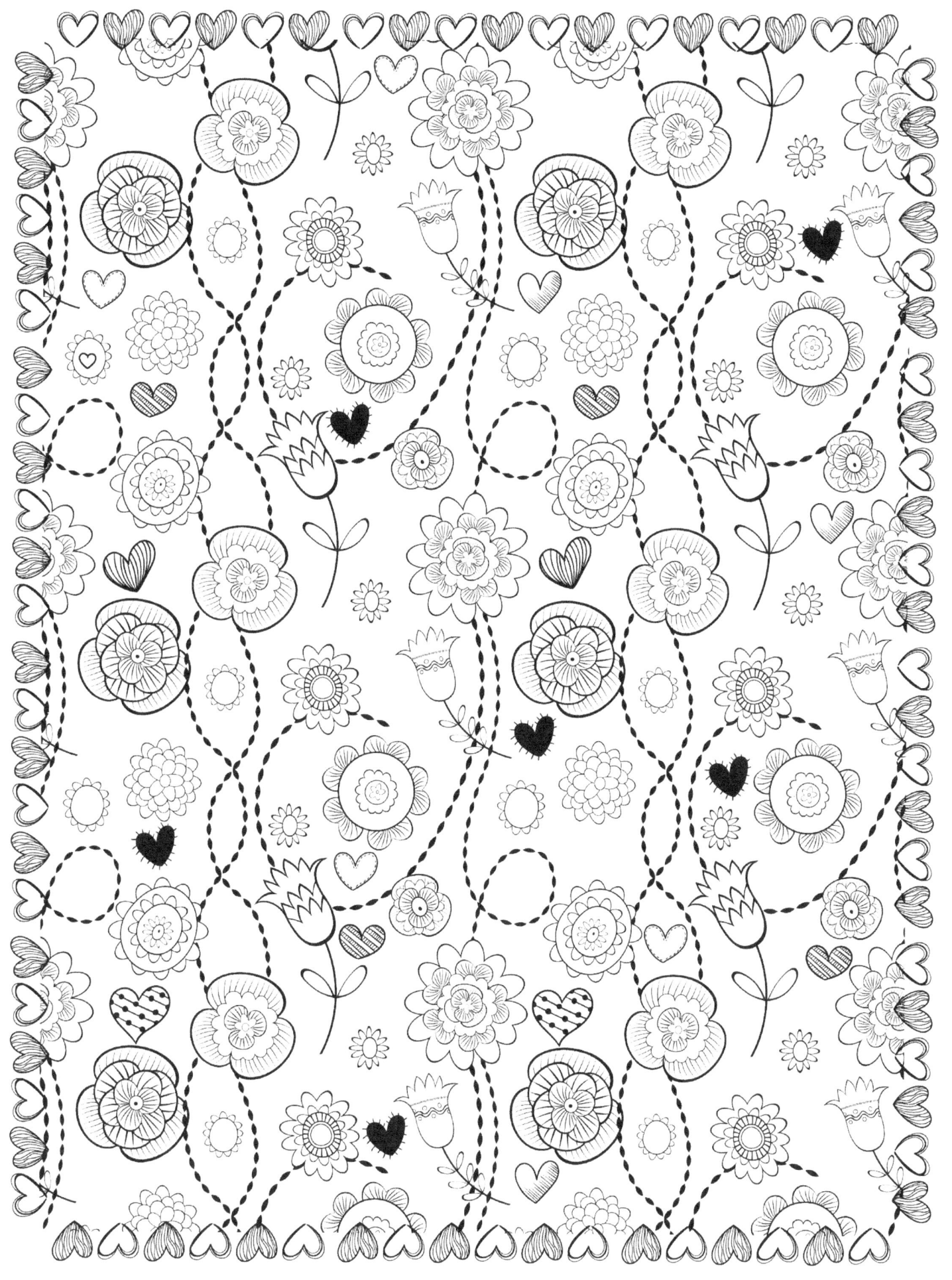

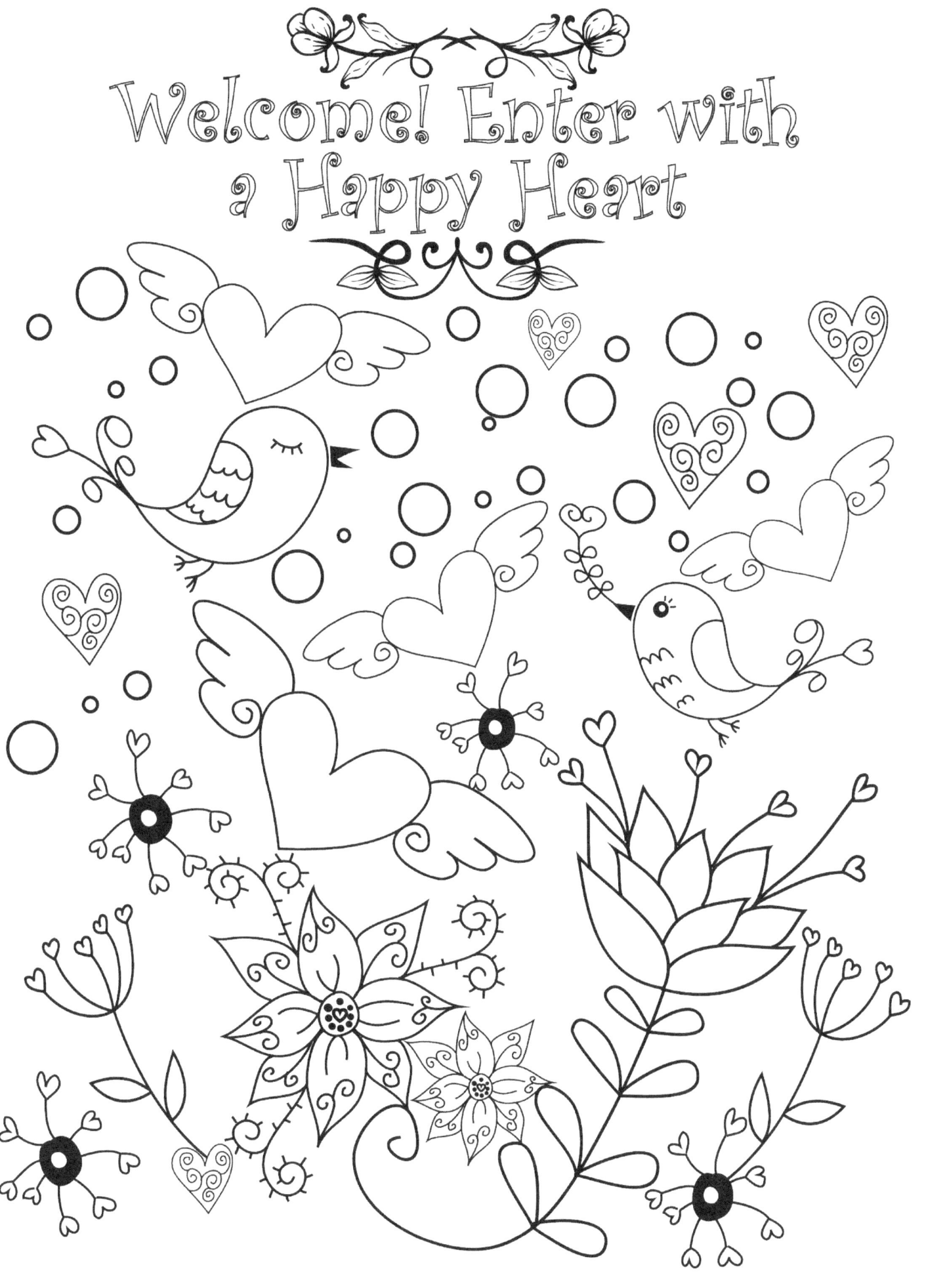

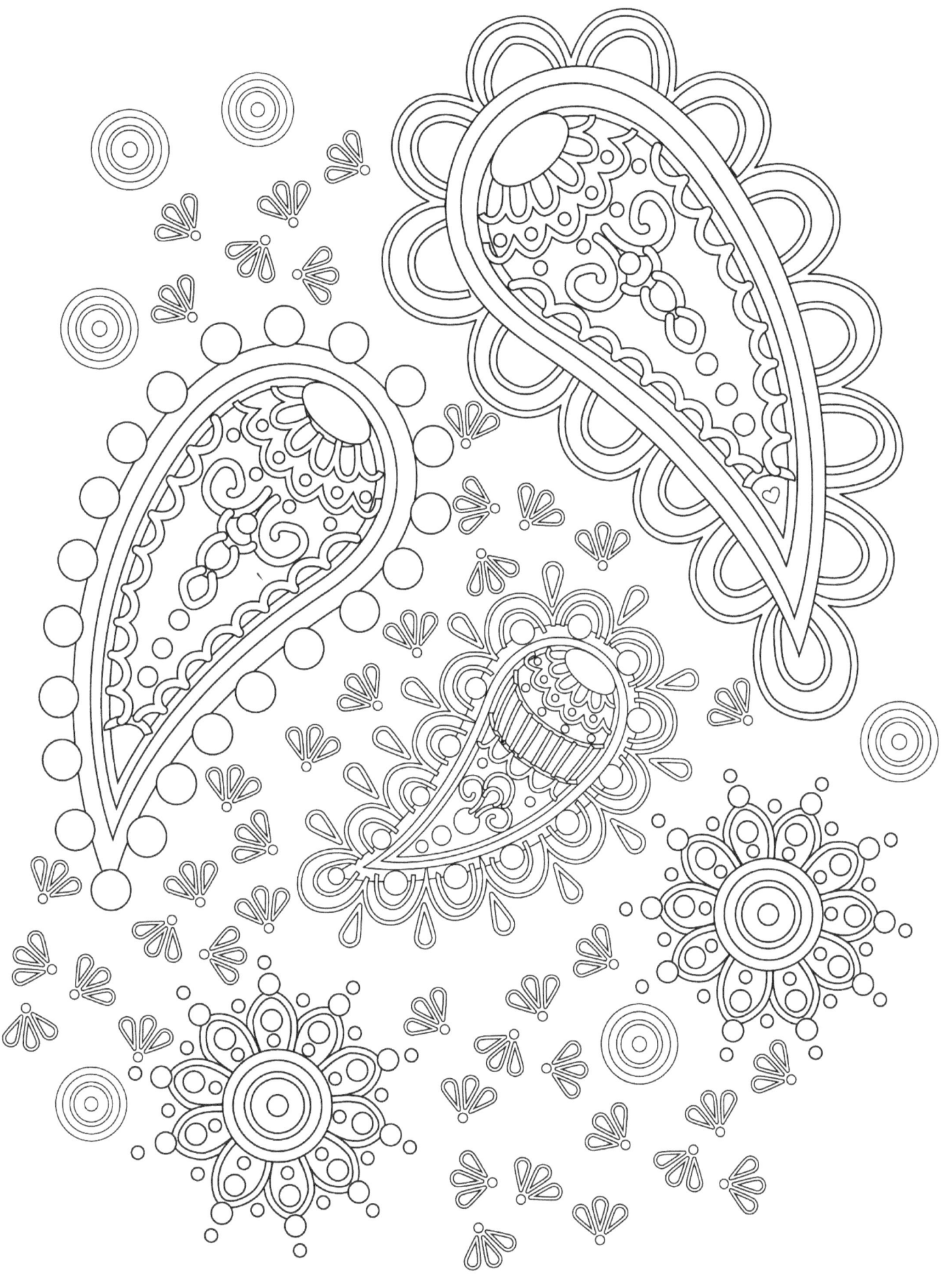

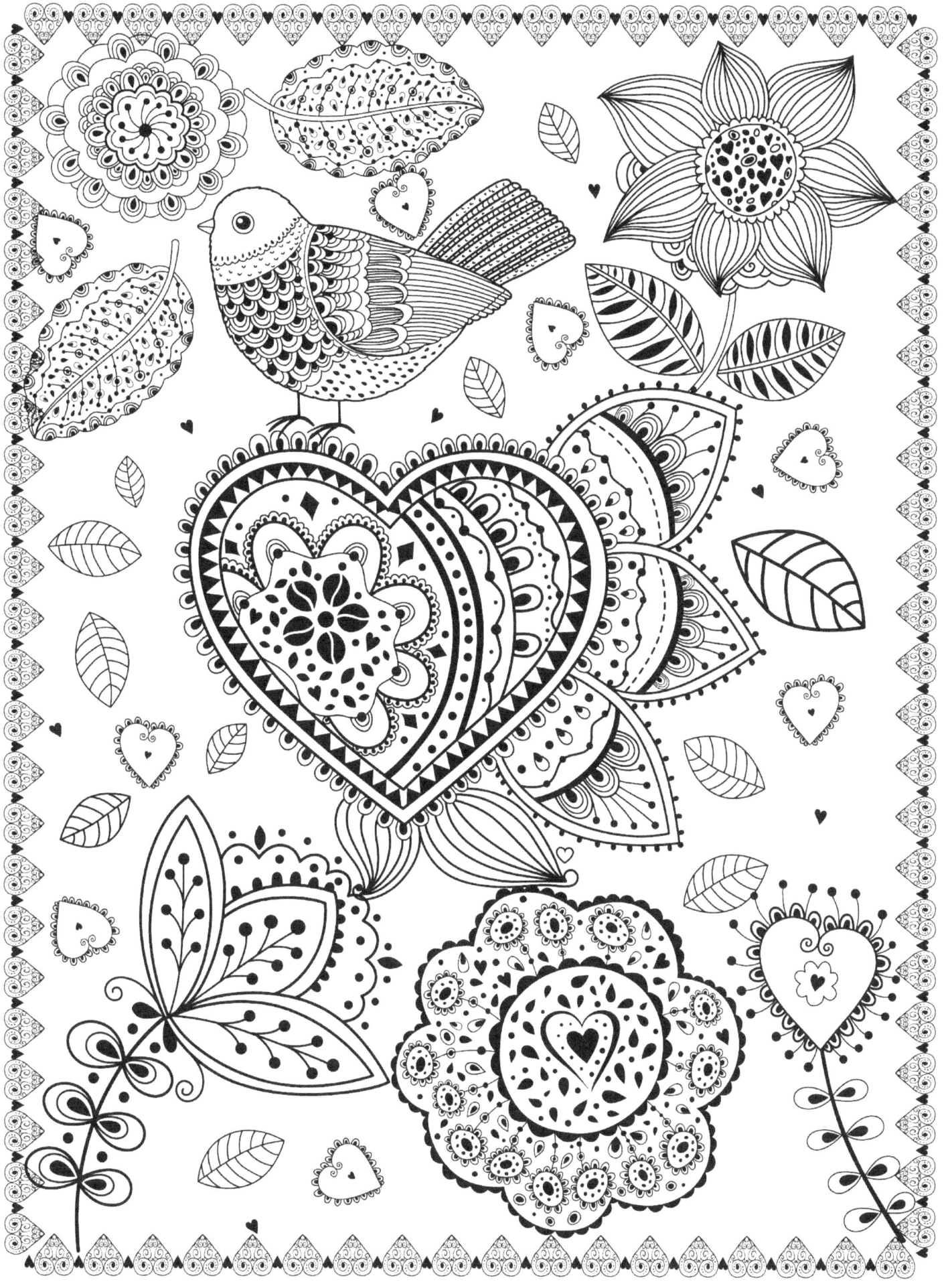

Happiness is in the Heart

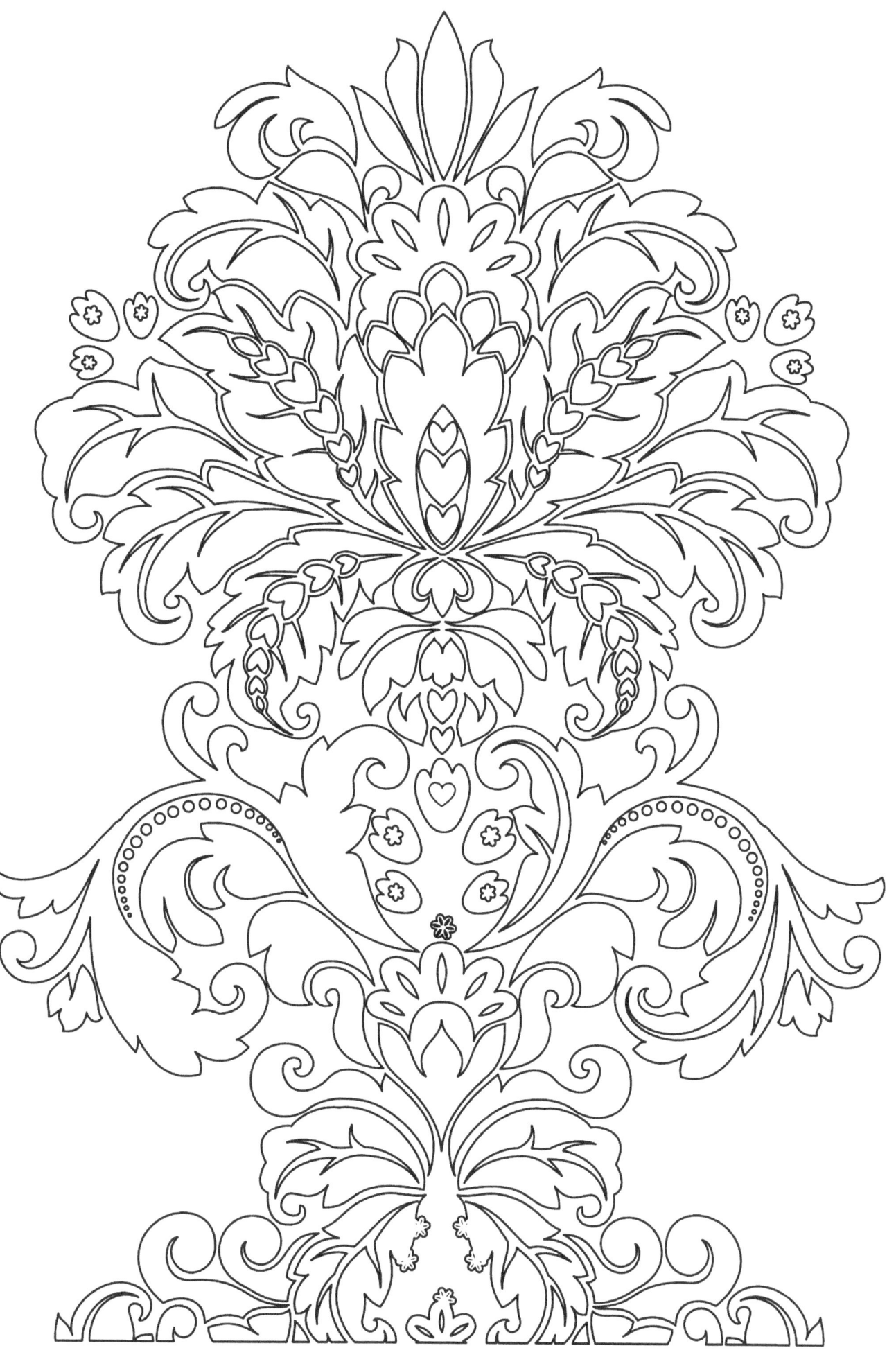

A Happy Heart
Makes the Face Cheerful

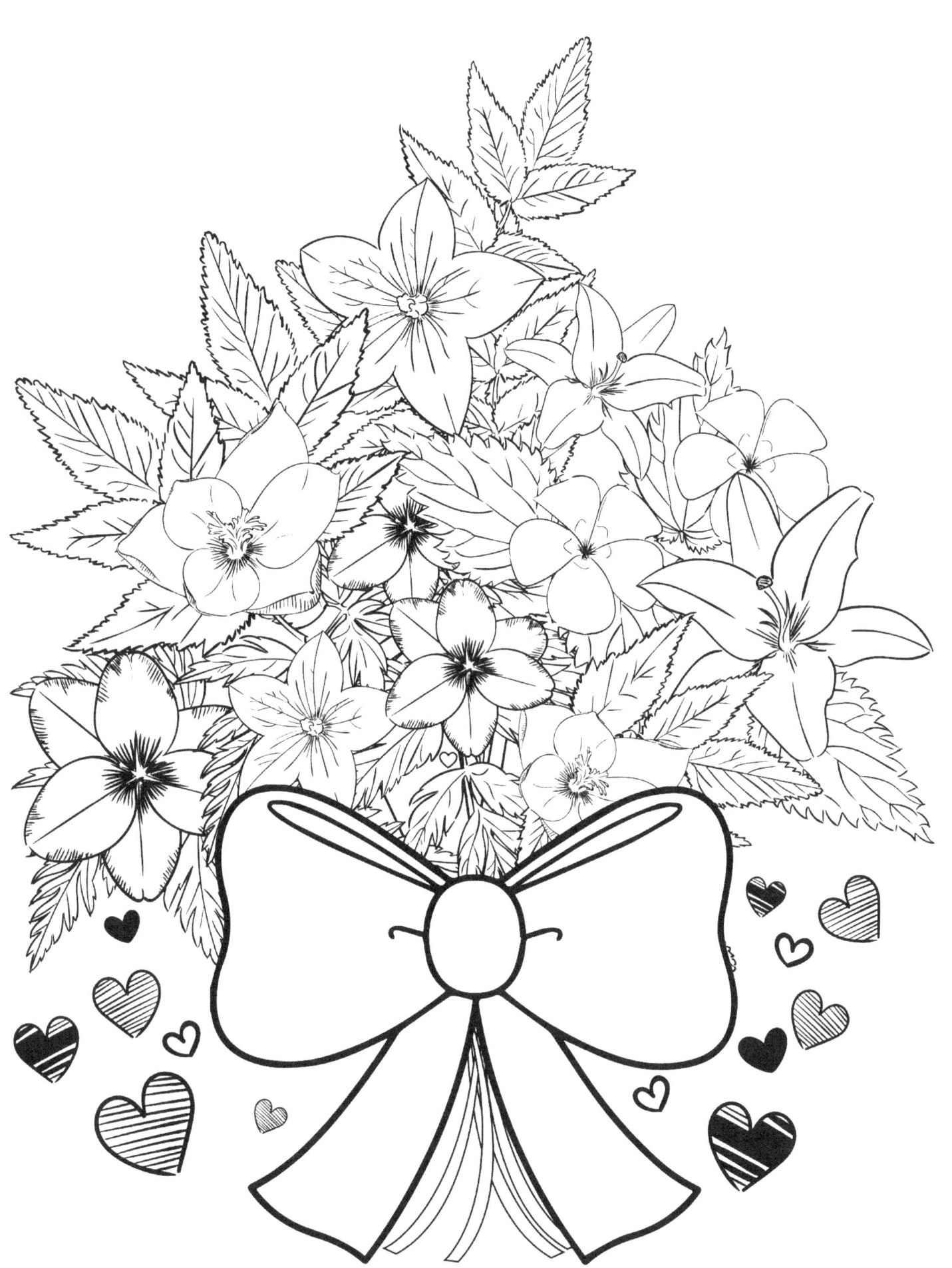

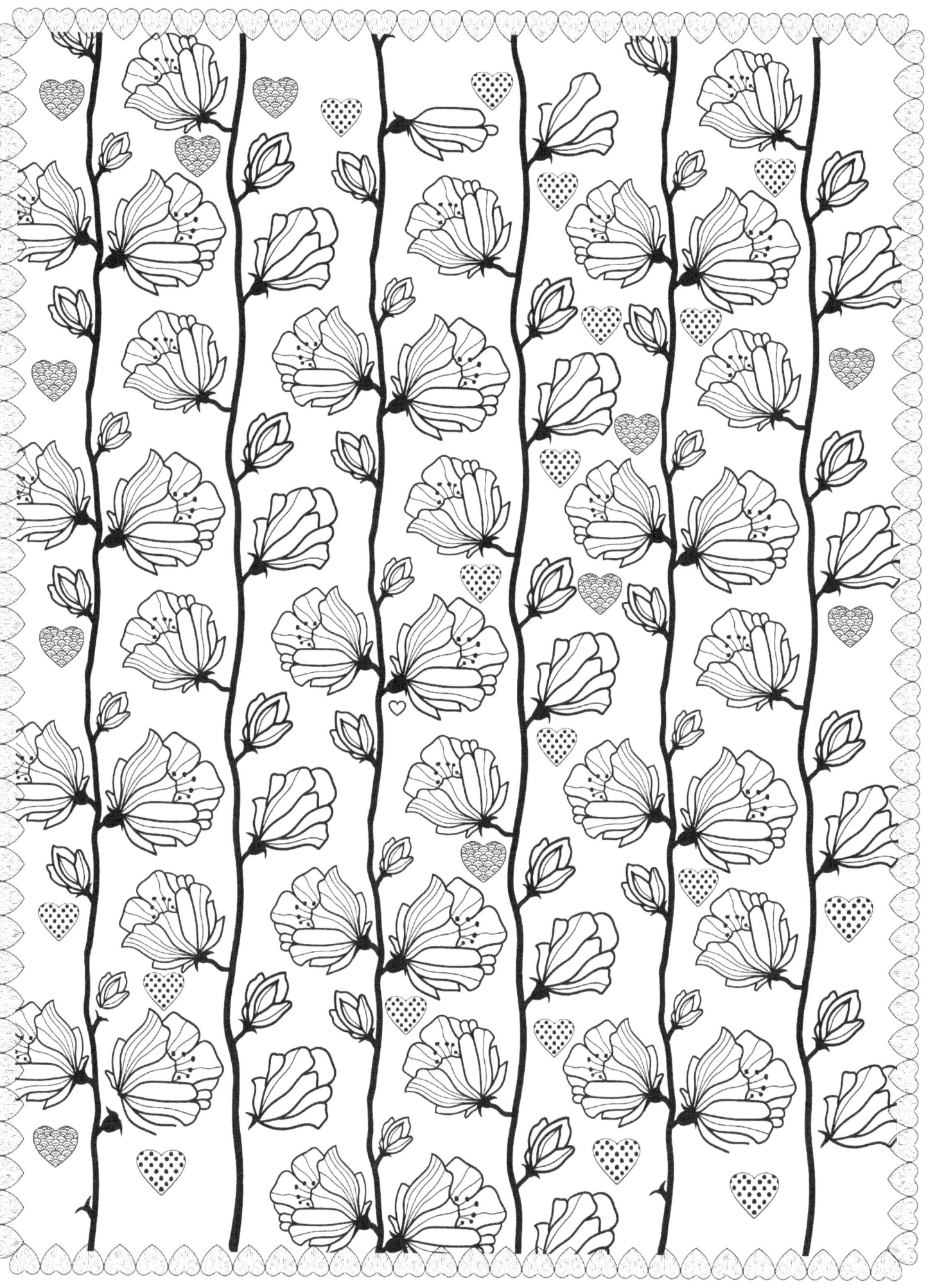

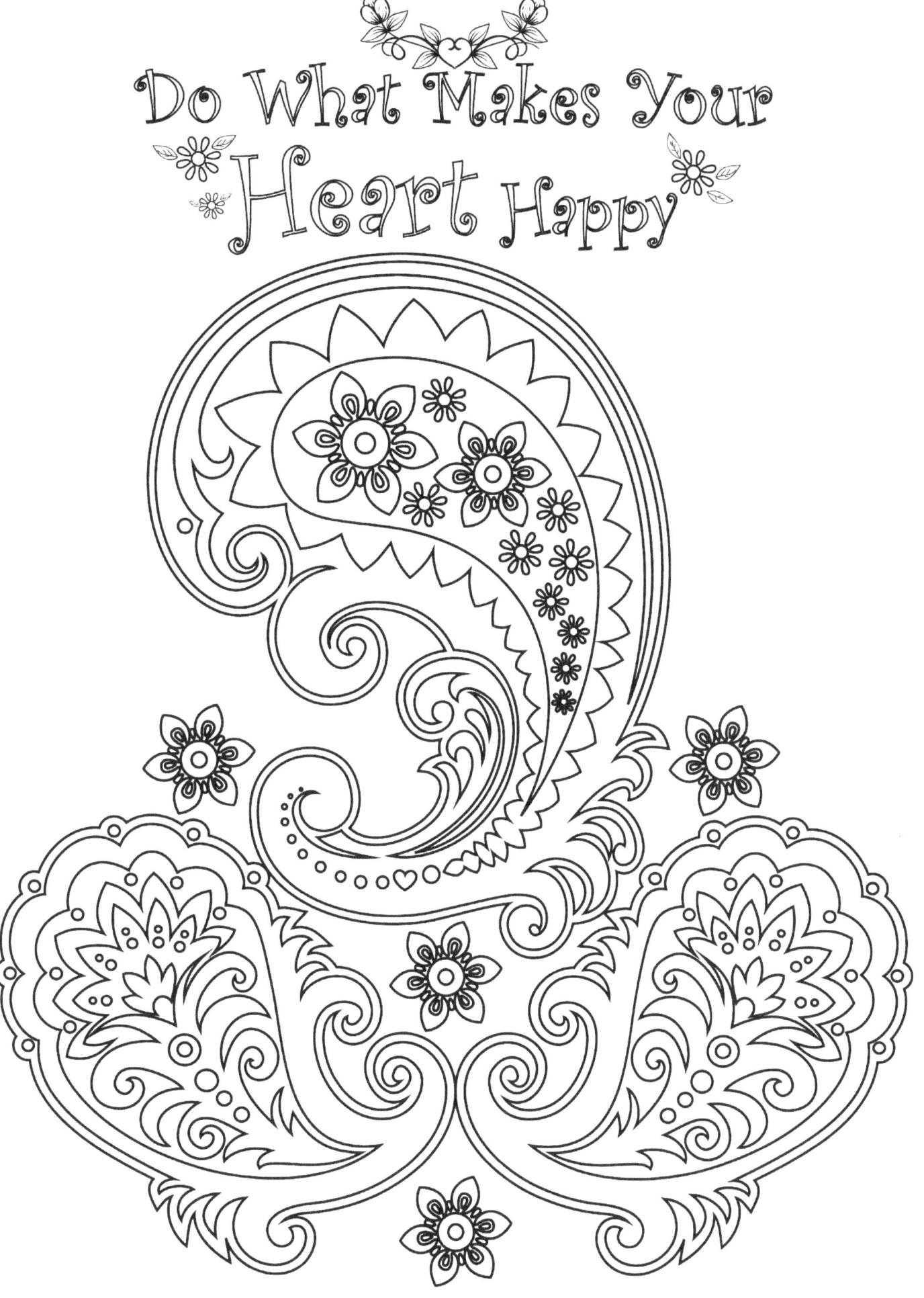

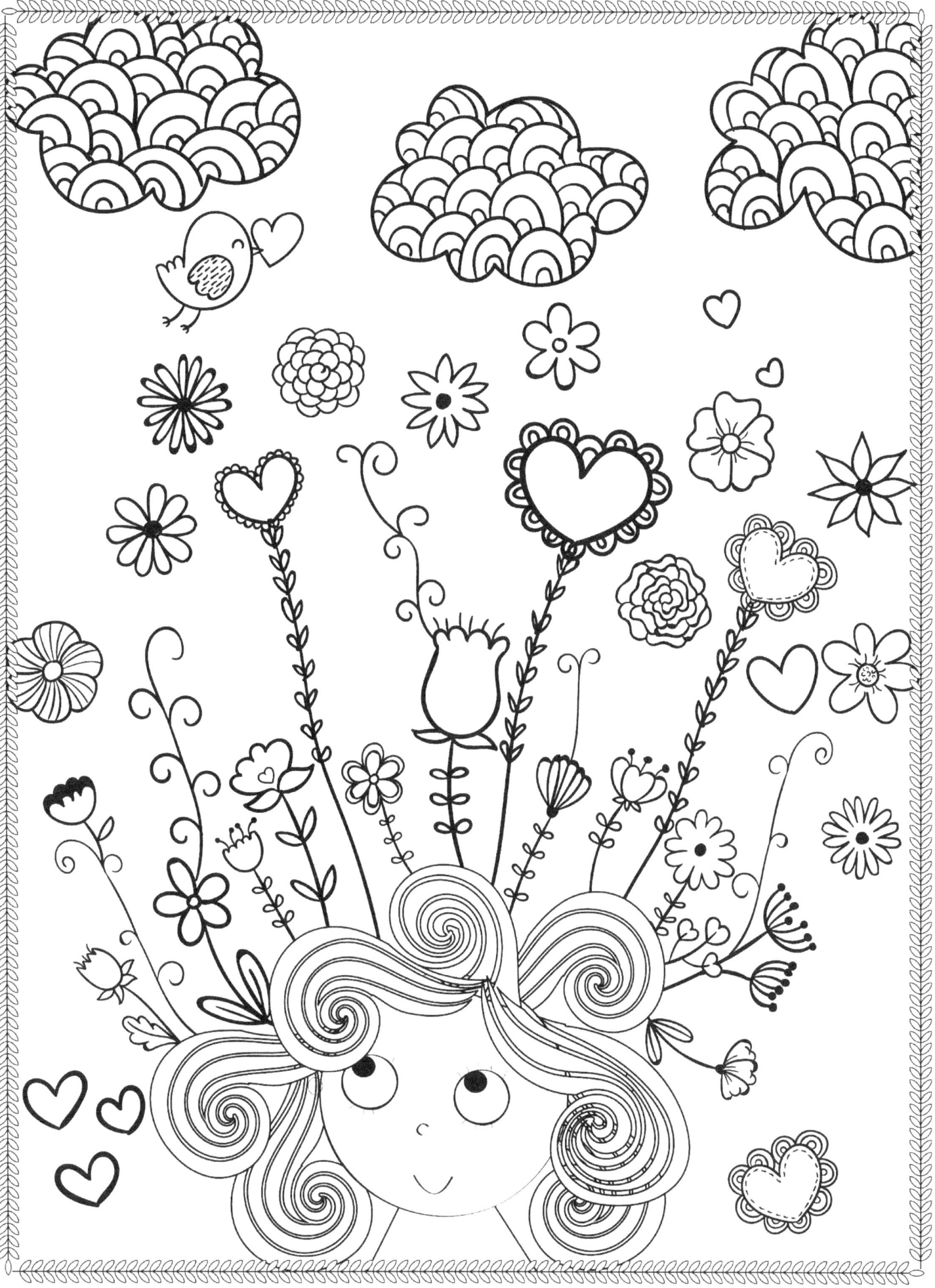

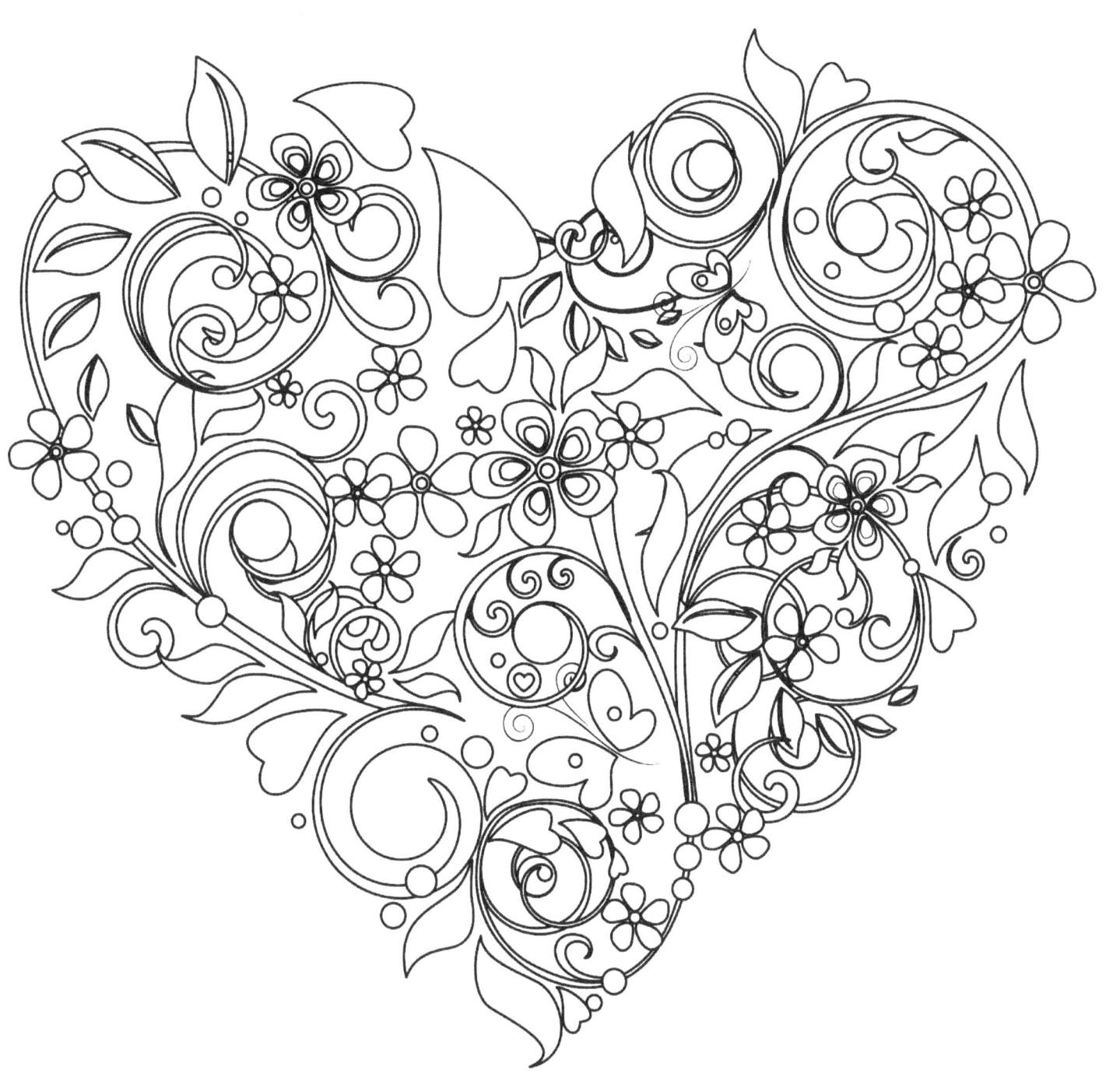

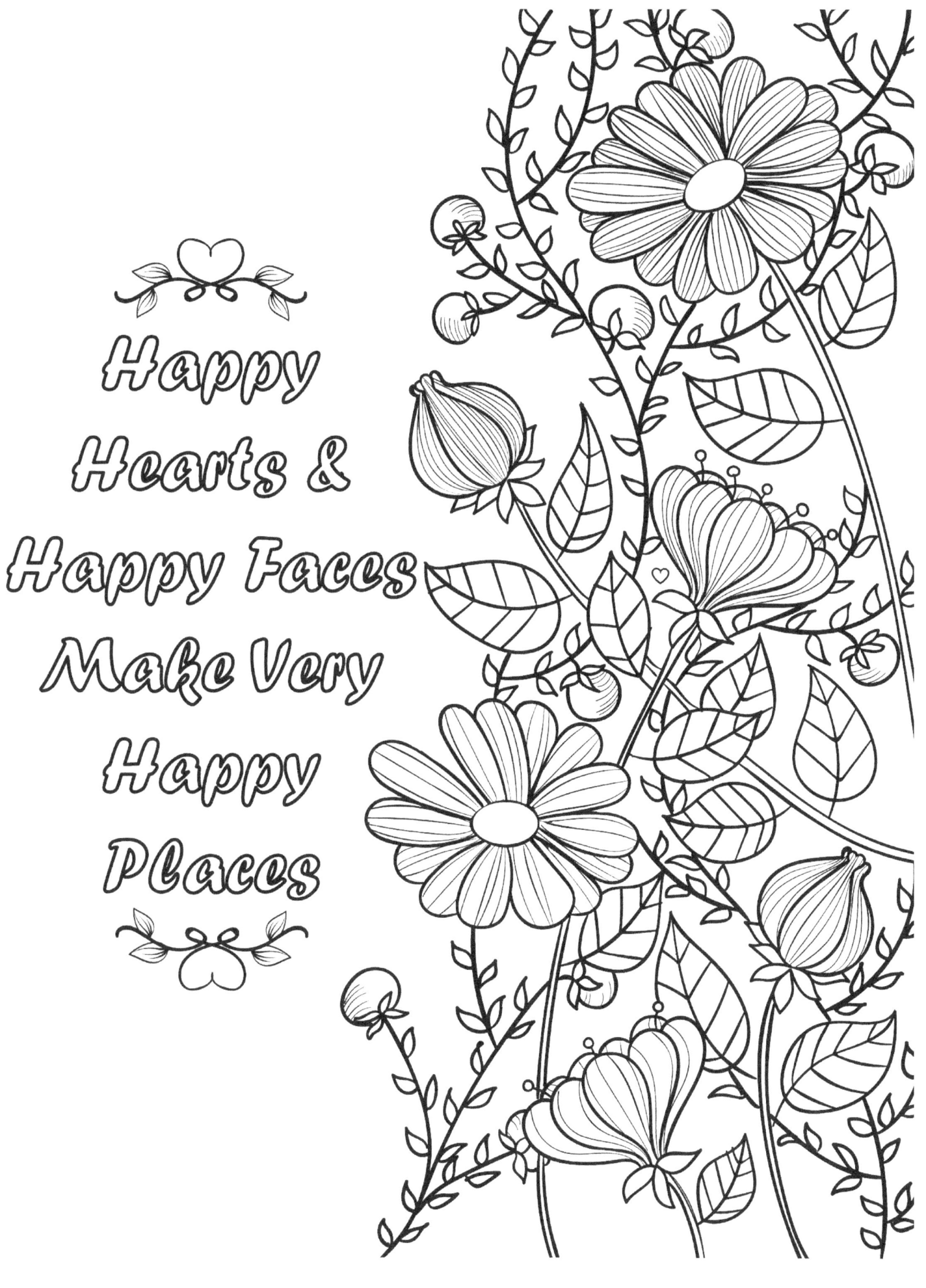

Happy
Hearts &
Happy Faces
Make Very
Happy
Places

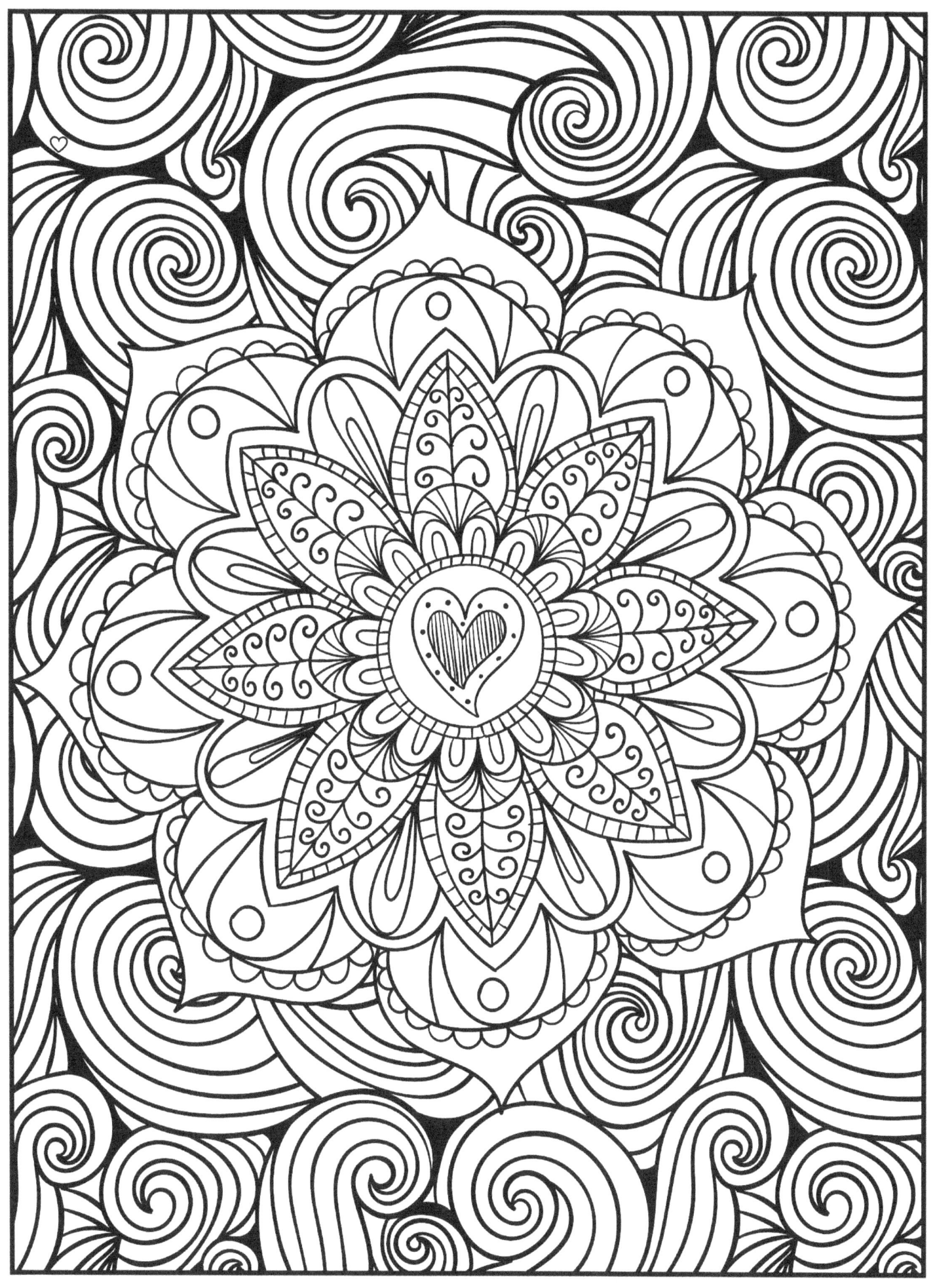

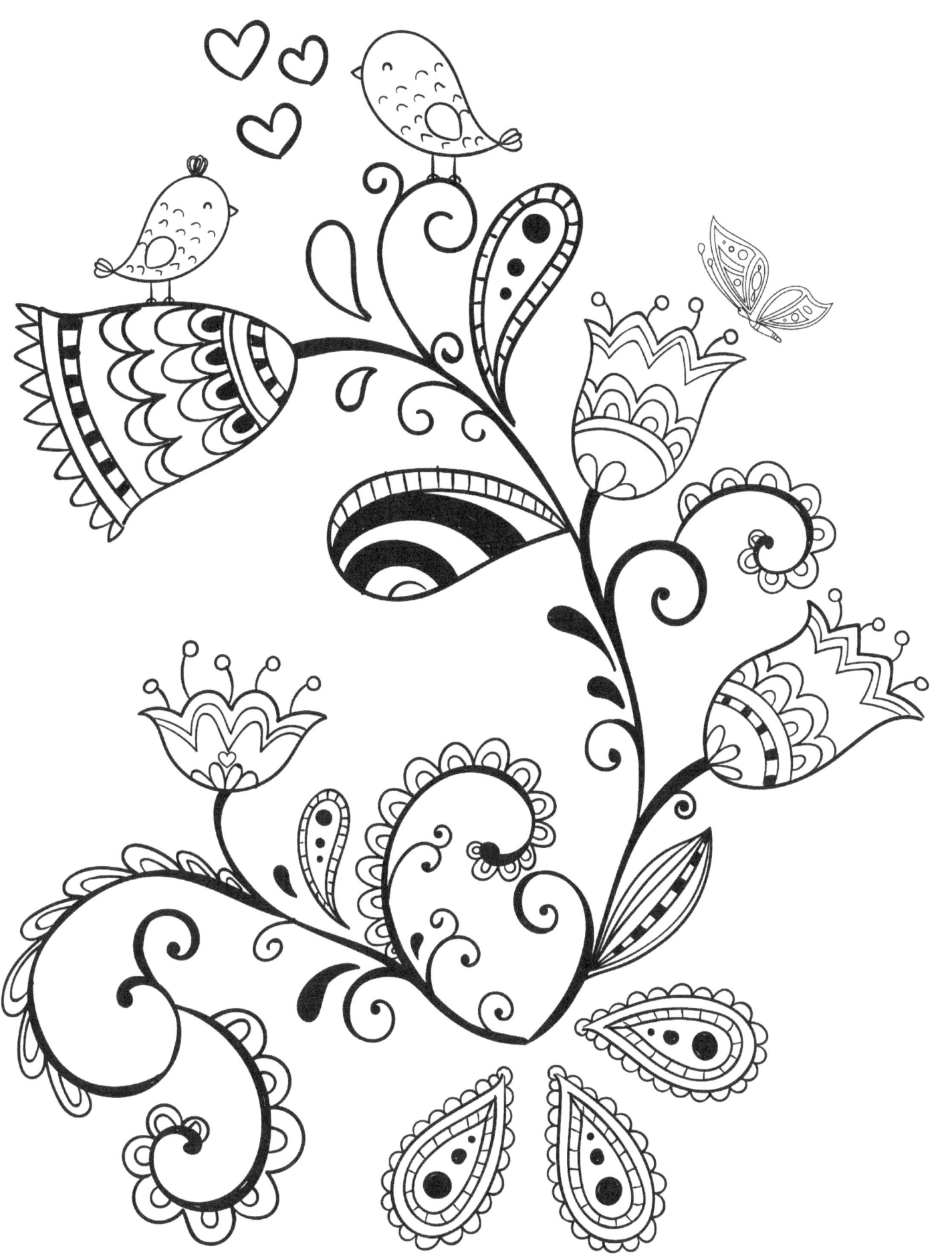

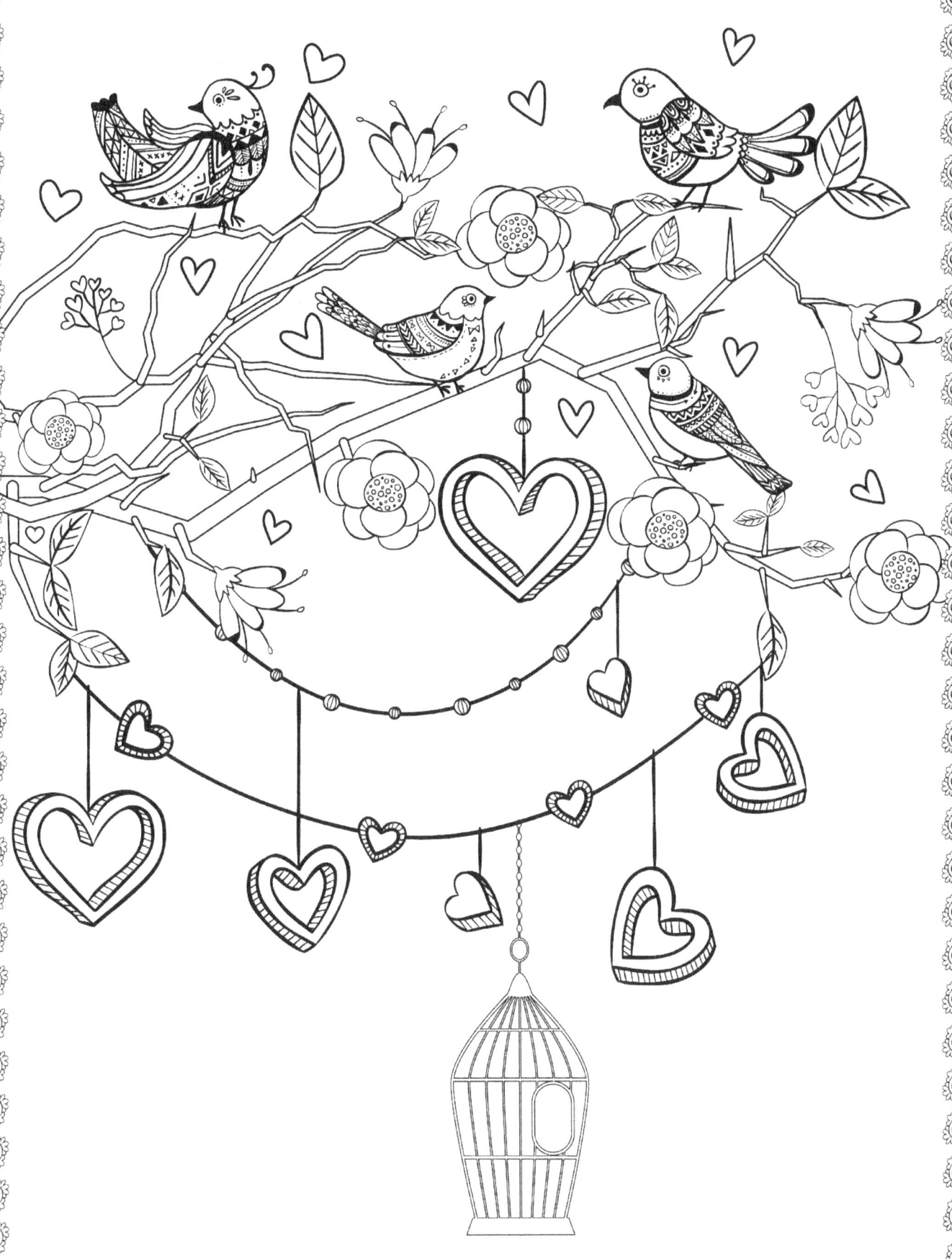

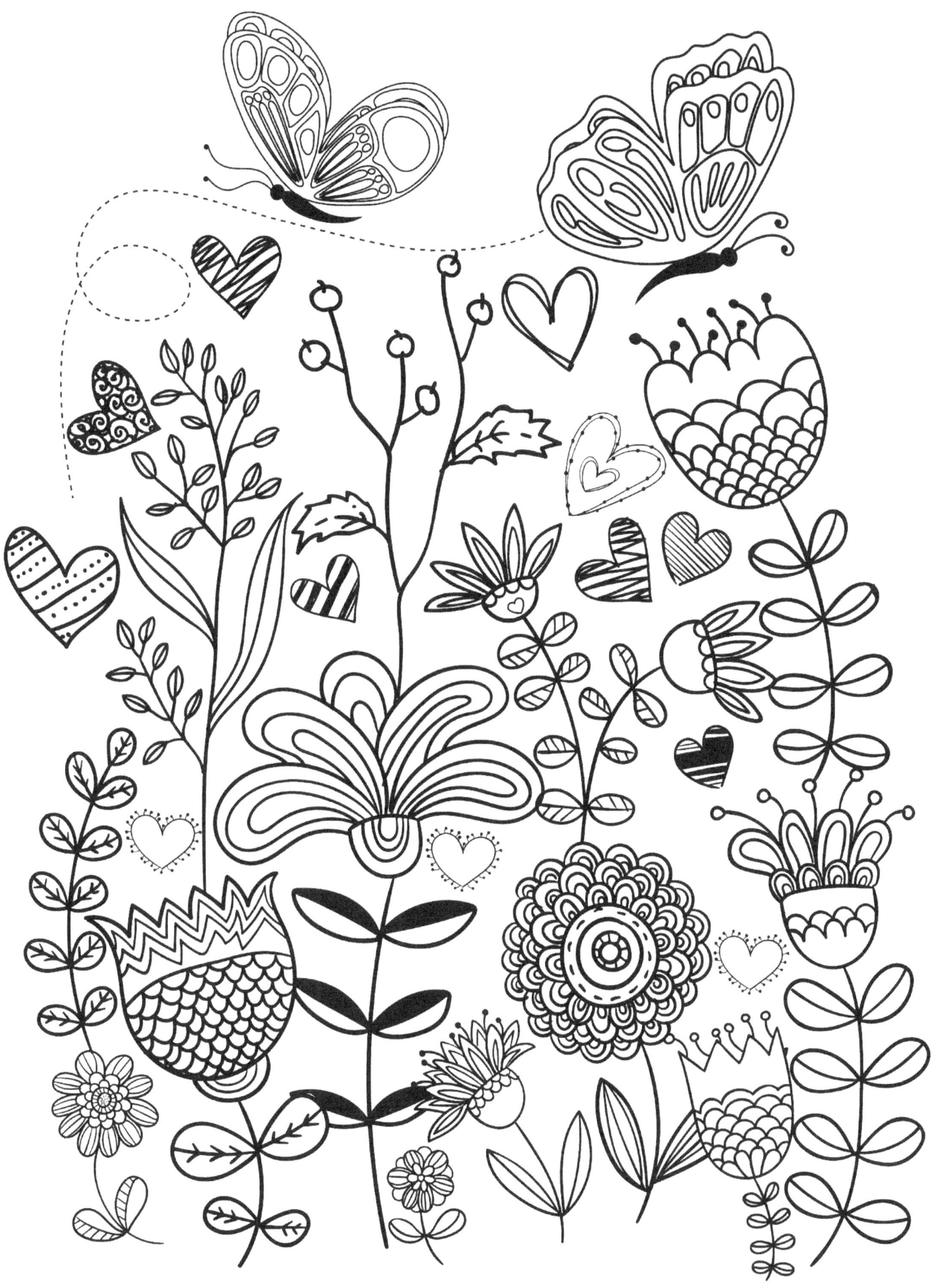

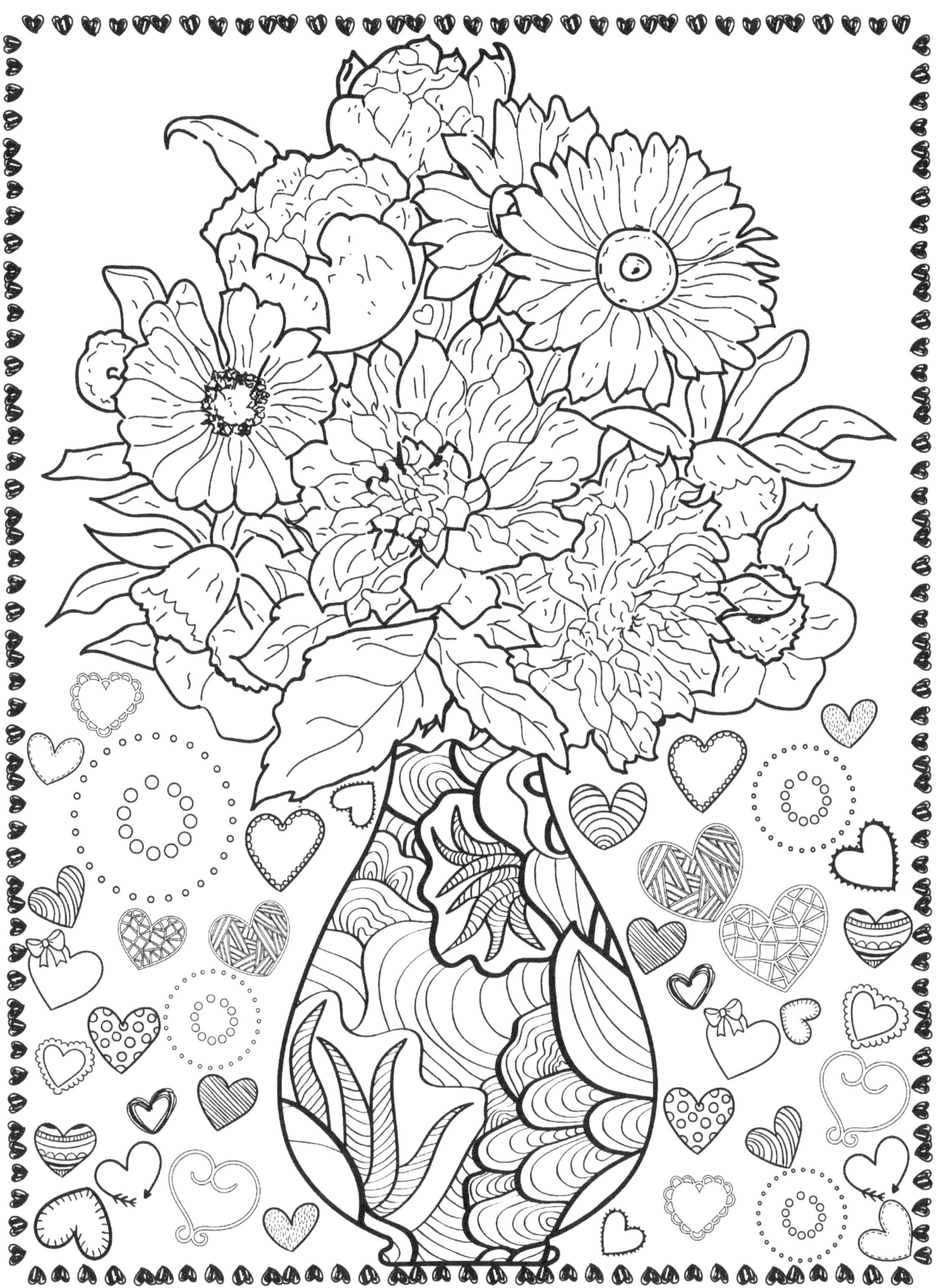

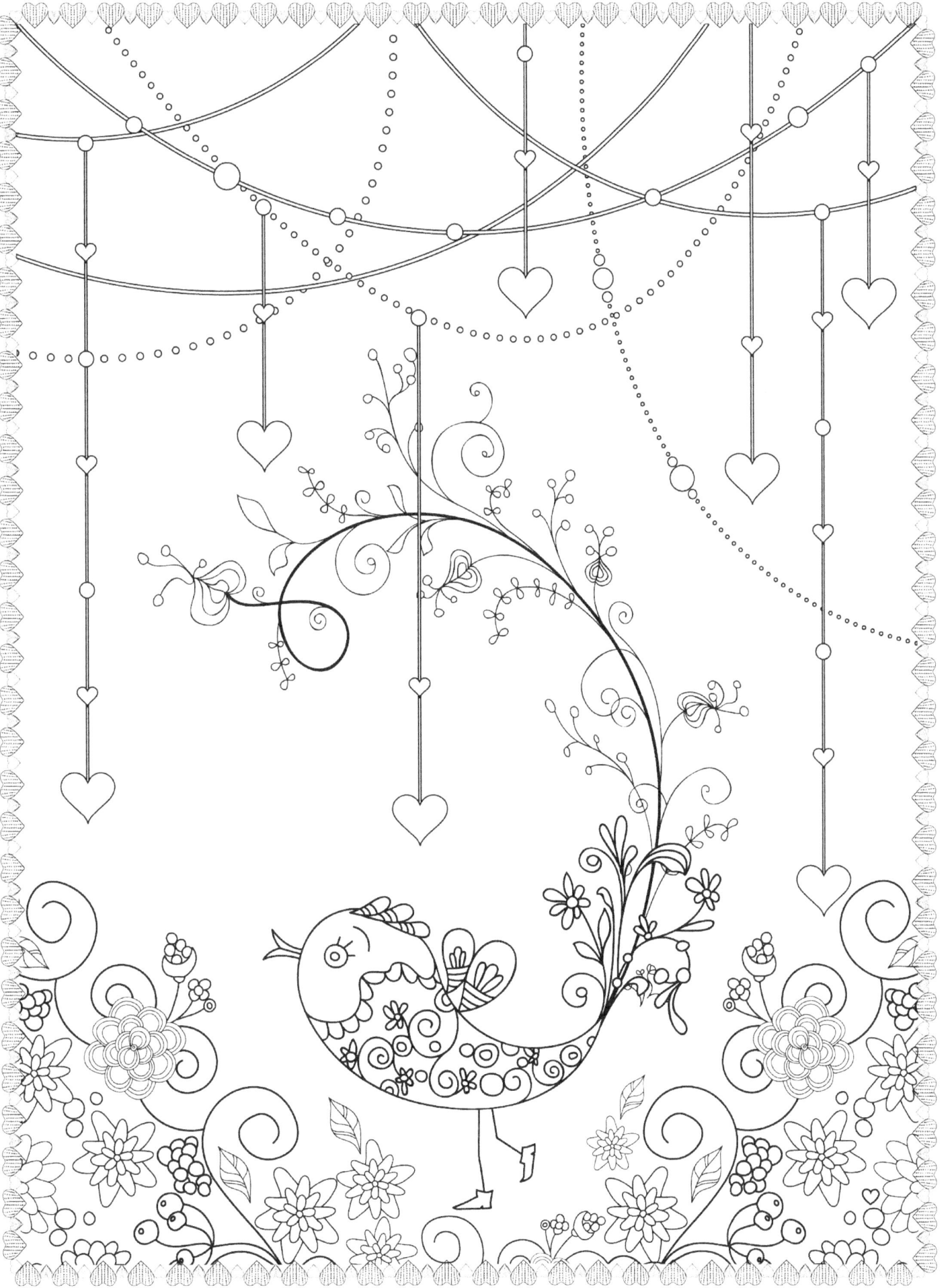

Follow your Heart

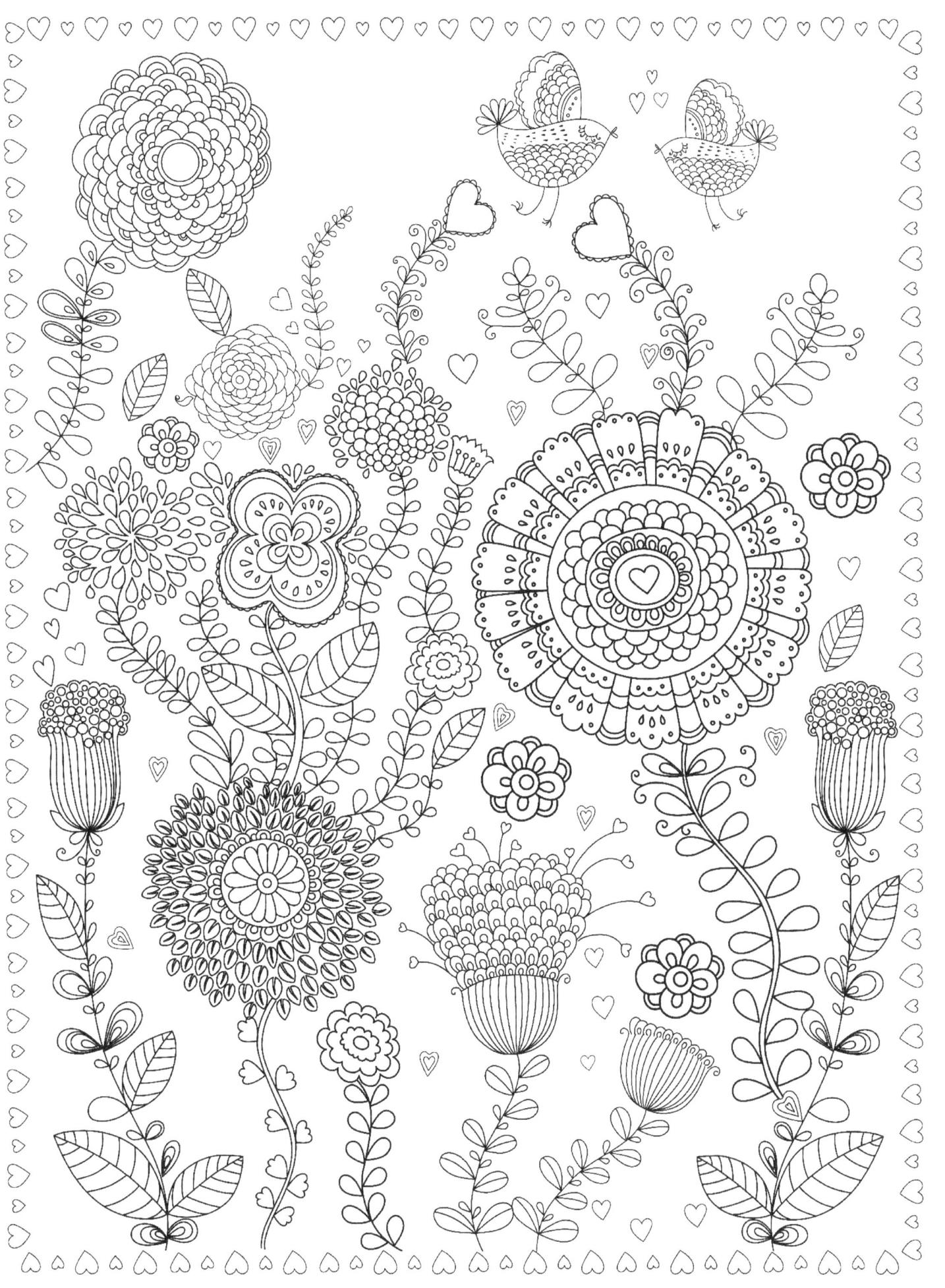

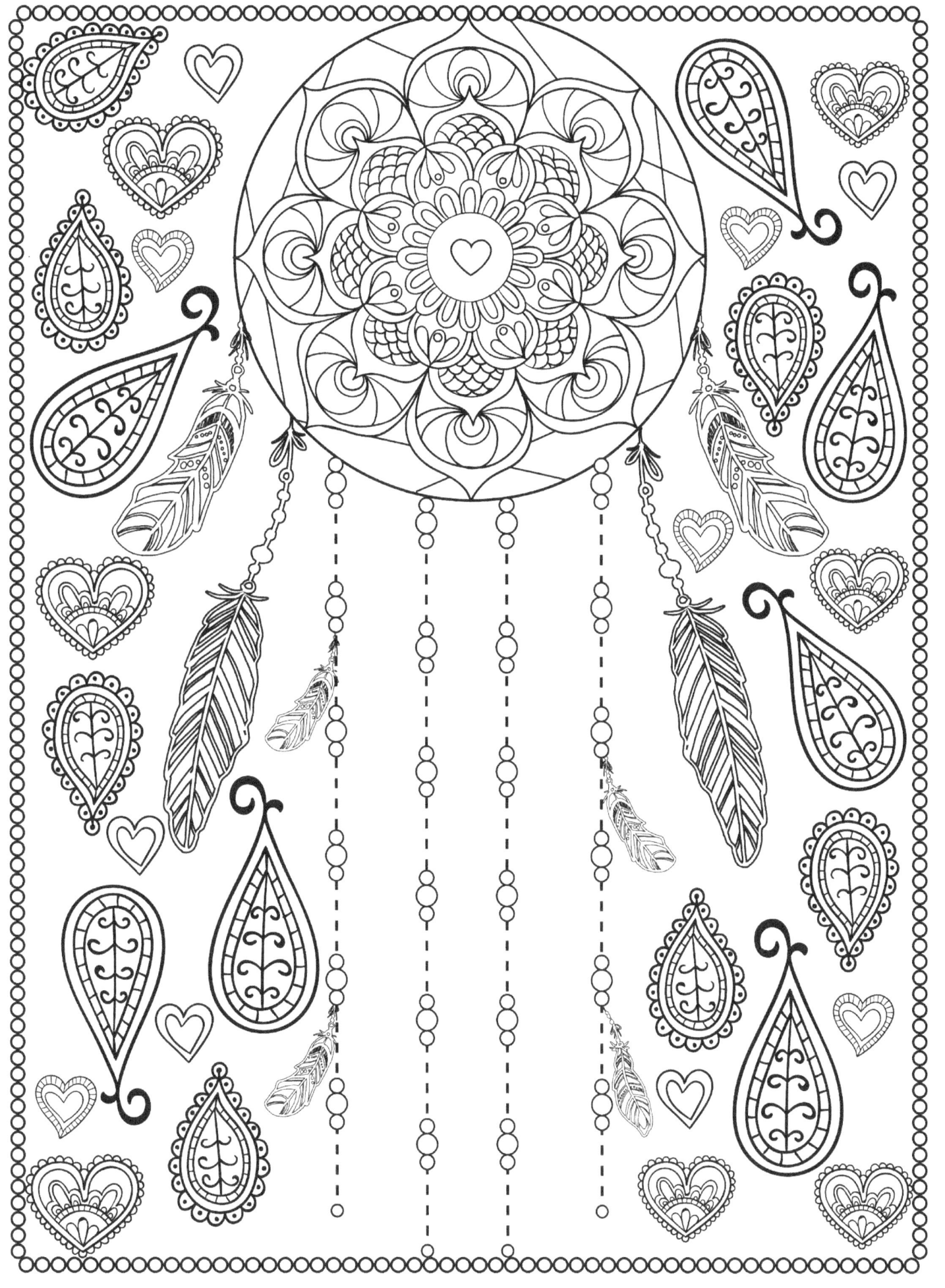

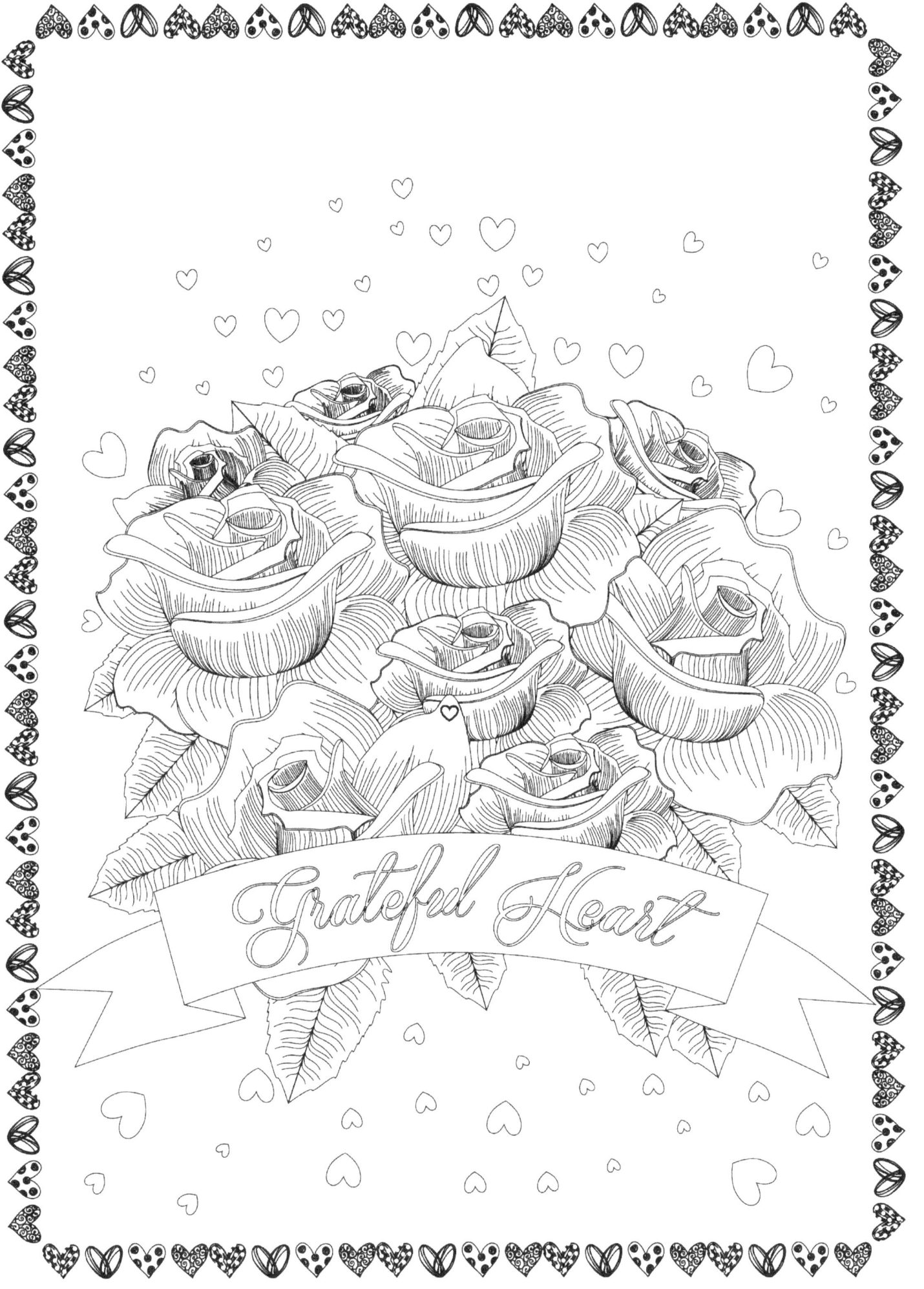

www.ingramcontent.com/pod-product-compliance
Lightning Source LLC
Chambersburg PA
CBHW080546190526
45169CB00007B/2660